1. Aberdeen
2. Aberdeenshi
3. Arran & Ayr:
4. Argyll
5. Southern Arg,
6. The Borders
7. The Cairngorms
8. Caithness & Sutherland
9. Dumfries and Galloway
10. Dundee & Angus
11. Edinburgh
12. Fife, Kinross & Clackmannan
13. Glasgow
14. Inverness
15. The Isle of Skye
16. Lanarkshire

21. Moray
22. Mull & Iona
23. Orkney
24. Orkney in Wartime
25. The Outer Hebrides
26. The City of Perth
27. Highland Perthshire
28. Ross & Cromarty
29. Royal Deeside
30. Shetland
31. Stirling & The Trossachs

The remaining four books, Caledonia, Distinguished Distilleries, Scotland's Mountains and Scotland's Wildlife feature locations throughout the country so are not included in the above list.

PICTURING SCOTLAND

THE BORDERS

COLIN NUTT
Author and photographer

2   The Royal Border Bridge carries the East Coast main line from London to Edinburgh across the River Tweed at Berwick. Opened in 1850, its 28 arches reach a height of 38m/125ft.

THE BORDERS

Welcome to the Borders!

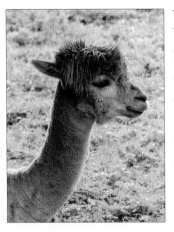

The glory of Scotland is the uncanny way its regions and counties are so diverse yet all are distinctively Scottish. So it is with the Borders: you know you are in Scotland and you know there is nowhere else in Scotland you can be. The modern-day region of Scottish Borders comprises the former counties of Berwickshire, Roxburghshire, Selkirkshire and Peeblesshire plus the southern part of Midlothian, yet these earlier entities have merged into a harmonious blend of scenery and settlement. That harmony is due in no small part to the dominance of the River Tweed and its tributaries such as the Teviot and Yarrow. As well as its defining role within the region, the Tweed also forms the actual and natural border between England and Scotland from Carham to Berwick.

Mention of Berwick leads to a word of explanation, for this book begins its journey through the Borders at this historically vital town, despite it being 'English' since 1482. Taken from Northumbria by the Scots in 1018, it was granted Royal Burgh status by King David I around 1124. This helped Berwick to grow into one of Scotland's wealthiest trading ports by the late 1200s. For the next 200 years its prosperity declined due to the repeated ravages brought upon it by the conflicts between Scotland and England. Worst of these was the genocide inflicted by Edward I in 1296 when at least 7,500 out of a population of 13,000 were massacred, making this one of the worst atrocities in the history of medieval Britain. During its strife-torn centuries it

4

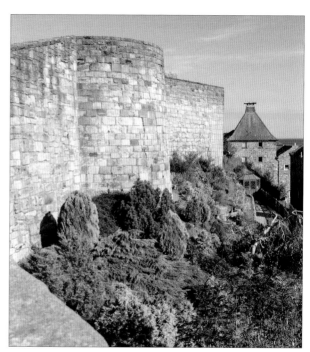

Left: Scotland begins here! This sign of welcome is at Carter Bar where the A68 breasts the summit between England and Scotland. Right: part of Berwick's town walls.   **5**

changed hands, on average, once every 15 years. As a result of its frontier status, it became one of the most fortified towns in Britain, leaving a legacy that is a major reason to visit the town today. Beginning at Berwick is a good way to make sense of the region's story.

An exploration of the Borders is a journey through Scotland's history. As part of the frontier with England, incursions, cattle-raiding, skirmishes and full-blown battles formed a centuries-long backdrop to daily life. Towerhouse castles like Neidpath near Peebles speak of this era. Later, when the thirst for strife declined, some of these castles evolved into more palatial dwellings, as demonstrated by Thirlestane Castle just outside Lauder. From the Georgian era to Edwardian times, country mansions like Mellerstain and Manderston appeared. The four great Border Abbeys of Dryburgh, Jedburgh, Kelso and Melrose, founded by King David I, survived their share of the region's troubles for centuries, only to be brought to final ruin by Henry VIII of England's

6   A view of Dryburgh Abbey. See also the front cover picture. Its rural location gives it a very different atmosphere from the urban settings of the other three principal Borders' Abbeys.

'Rough Wooing' in the 16th century. The fertility of the land in the valleys is evident both in terms of arable and livestock farms. The textiles industry gave rise to towns like Hawick and Galashiels, still home to leading brands even if some of the manufacturing is done elsewhere.

So this book begins its journey in Berwick and embarks on a broadly circular tour of the region, during the course of which it aims to present the huge range of sites and scenery that give the Borders their special charm. Travelling in a clockwise direction means we begin by tracing the border with England as far as the Cheviot Hills, where the Pennine Way terminates at Kirk Yetholm. After dipping south towards the border with Dumfries and Galloway, we turn north through the hillscapes between numerous dales, coming within sight of Lanarkshire before turning west to zigzag our way back across to the North Sea coast. Whether our interests lie in architecture and townscapes or landscapes and rural rides, the Borders deliver a host of images that combine to make a most memorable tour.

The town of Duns, where the medieval theologian and philosopher John Duns Scotus was born c.1265.

8   The inviting panorama of the Borders from Carter Bar. This northerly view gives an idea of the terrain and scenery that waits to be explored. In 1575 Carter Bar was the scene of the Raid of the Redeswir

This was the last major battle between the Kingdom of England and the Kingdom of Scotland.

10 This picture makes it clear that Berwick-upon-Tweed is an important bridging point! The Old Bridge in the foreground was built from 1611 to 1624. The middle, larger-span road bridge dates to 1928.

Berwick's town walls provide some good viewpoints from which to appreciate the town centre. 11
Where the wall crosses Castlegate, this view looks down Marygate to the Town Hall.

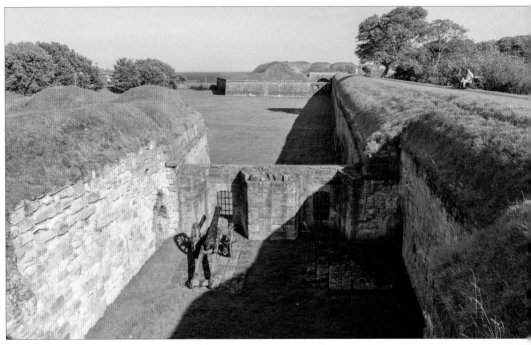

12 Huge bastions still surround Berwick on all sides except the south, where the River Tweed provides a natural defence. This is part of the northern ramparts, with cannon still in place. Given Berwick's

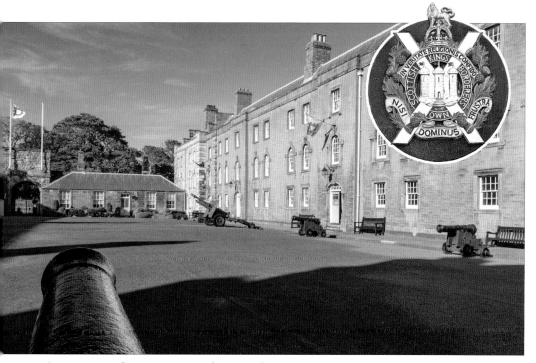

location it's no surprise that it is garrisoned: Ravensdowne Barracks are the oldest in Britain, begun in 1717. Inset: the crest of the King's Own Scottish Borderers, based here from 1881 to 1964.

14 A few miles west of Berwick, on the banks of the river Tweed, is Paxton House. Built by the Adam brothers in 1758, it is perhaps the finest example of 18th century Palladian Country houses in Britain

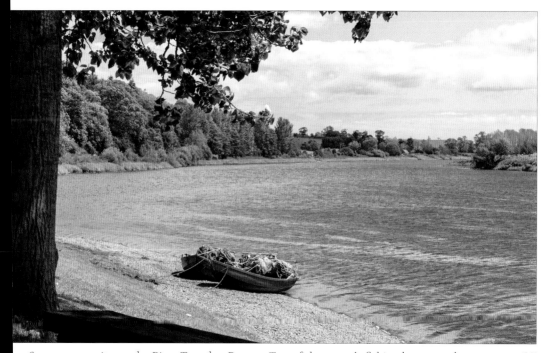

Summer serenity on the River Tweed at Paxton. Two of the estate's fishing boats are drawn up on the bank. From its source at Tweed's Well the river flows for 156km/97 miles through the Borders.

THIS STONE WAS PRESENTED
TO THE BURGH OF COLDSTREAM
BY THE COLDSTREAM REGIMENT
OF FOOT GUARDS ON THE DAY
ON WHICH THEY WERE PROUD TO RECEIVE
THE FREEDOM OF THE BURGH
10TH AUGUST 1968

IT WAS FROM NEAR HERE
ON 1ST JANUARY 1660 THAT
GENERAL MONCK CROSSED
THE RIVER TWEED TO START
HIS MARCH TO LONDON
CULMINATING IN THE
RESTORATION OF
KING CHARLES II

16 Continuing westwards, the village of Coldstream is situated at the lowest fording point on the Tweed. This is Henderson Park, location of the Coldstream Guards Stone (inset).

Coldstream Museum's Guards Gallery, pictured here, tells the story of the Coldstream Guards. **17** The origins of the regiment go back to 1650, when it was formed at the instruction of Oliver Cromwell.

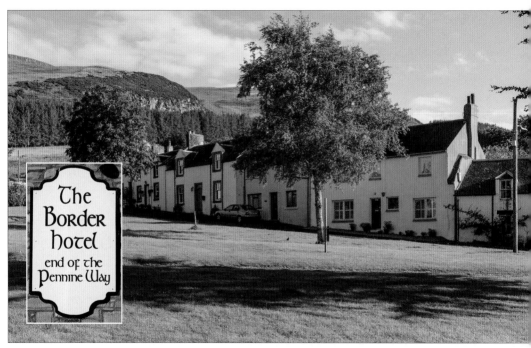

The Border hotel
end of the Pennine Way

18 Southwards now, and an evening view of the village of Kirk Yetholm, set against the slopes of the Cheviot Hills. Inset: Kirk Yetholm is at the end of the Pennine Way.

The attractive village of Town Yetholm in autumn. The name Yetholm means the 'place at the gate', **19** from the old Scots 'yett' meaning a gate and 'holm' or 'ham', the Anglo-Saxon for a settlement.

20 Near Yetholm, the shadows lengthen over a pleasing agricultural scene illustrating the mixed nature of farming in the Borders, with arable and livestock in neighbouring fields.

Travelling north-west from Yetholm we reach the impressive town of Kelso. Here in The Square, **21** the Town Hall stands beyond the 'Kelsae Stane', a new sculpture by Jake Harvey, unveiled in 2014.

22 Kelso boasts the largest market square in Scotland, the scale of which can be appreciated in this picture. The grandest building on the square is the Cross Keys Hotel, built in 1760 as a coaching inn.

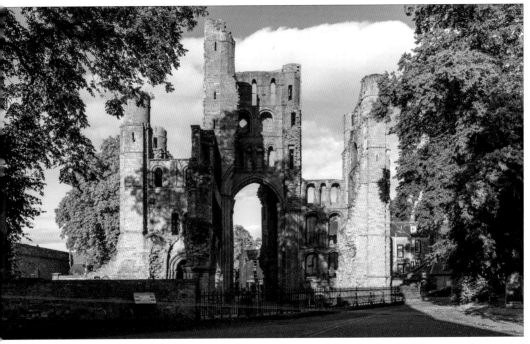

Little remains of Kelso Abbey today, yet the stature of what still stands gives a clear clue to its former **23** grandeur. Built with two crossings and two towers, its layout was also unique in Scotland.

24 Floors Castle is built on a natural terrace overlooking the River Tweed, facing the Cheviot Hills, and is the home of the Roxburghe Family. It is based on a tower house which was added to by

William Adam from 1721. William Playfair remodelled the castle between 1837 and 1847. The result is a romantic fairytale castle with its roofscape of turrets, pinnacles and cupolas.

26 The Walled Garden at Floors Castle is a wonderful treat for anyone who enjoys the delights of spectacular herbaceous borders and expertly tended shrubs and plants of all types.

Returning to Kelso, more floral flair at the War Memorial gardens, just along Bridge Street from The 27
Square. Viewed from the other end, they provide a lovely foreground to the remains of Kelso Abbey.

28 Laburnum tunnel at Monteviot House Gardens. Extending to some 30 acres, the gardens include a formal rose garden, herb garden, herbaceous perennial river garden and an Oriental-style water garden

Continuing south into Jedburgh, first stop is the Castle Jail, a 19th-century Howard Reform prison **29** built on the site of a 12th-century castle. Today it is a museum that recreates prison life in the 1800s.

30 Now with the Jail behind us, this is the reverse view down Castle Gate which ends at Market Place in the centre of Jedburgh (see opposite page). Looking at the immaculate state of Jedburgh's Market

...ace today, it is hard to imagine what life must have been like in the strife-torn Middle Ages.
suffered attack or occupation 11 times from 1296 to 1548.

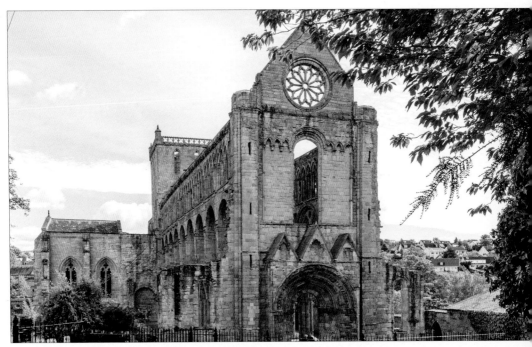

32 Jedburgh is the most intact of the 'big four' abbeys with its virtually complete nave, tower and north transept. This is astonishing given the number of times it was attacked during the Anglo-Scottish war

Left: visitors enjoy the peaceful atmosphere of the abbey. Right: Jedburgh's Mercat Cross is a work **33** of art that makes a striking centrepiece at the heart of the town.

34 This is the house where Mary, Queen of Scots, stayed during a visit to Jedburgh in 1566. Today the house contains a unique collection of objects and pictures that give an insight into her tragic life.

Our most southerly point is Hermitage Castle, which stands in lonely isolation about five miles north of Newcastleton. The dark clouds reflect its reputation as 'guardhouse of the bloodiest valley in Britain'.

36 Hawick is a substantial town with a population of over 14,000, making it one of the largest in the Borders. Its growth was based on the textiles industry, which remains important.

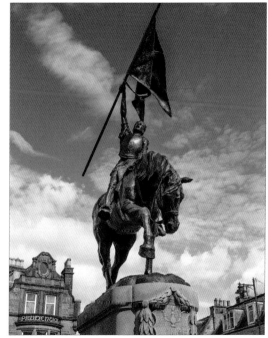

Left: the imposing tower of Hawick's Town Hall. Right: statue commemorating an event in 1514 **37** when Hawick lads fought off a raid by English troops, capturing the Hexham Banner in the process.

38 In the centre of Hawick, the 16th-century Black Tower of Drumlanrig is incorporated into this building, which houses the Borders Textile Towerhouse Museum. Opposite: Hand Stocking Frame in the museum

Above right: to mark the 500th anniversary of the event referred to on p.37, the 'Return from Hornshole' **39**
Monument was set up in 2014 to recall the captured flag being handed over to the townspeople.

40 The sweeping landscape of Ettrickdale, west of Hawick. This view, a few miles south-west of Ettrickbridge, exemplifies Borders scenery as the land rises towards the hills that line the western

...dge of the region. The poet and novelist James Hogg ('The Ettrick Shepherd', 1770-1835) ...ailed from this dale and is buried in the churchyard at Ettrick, a few miles further on.

42 Left: Angela Hunter's statue depicts William of Rule 'turning' an angry bull to save the life of Robert the Bruce. The surname 'Turnbull' originates from this incident. Right: a heron on Slitrig Water, Hawick.

Leaving Hawick behind we now head for the 'wild west' of the Borders. This scene, from a viewpoint 43
above the village of Roberton, looks to the south and captures a hill farm on a day of changing light.

44 A long-abandoned farm building in Ettrickdale shows nature reclaiming the land for itself. As the tree grows, it is steadily demolishing the stonework.

Traversing another ridge of hills we head north into the next dale, where the Yarrow Water, **45** seen here near the Gordon Arms, flows for 13 miles from St Mary's Loch to the Tweed.

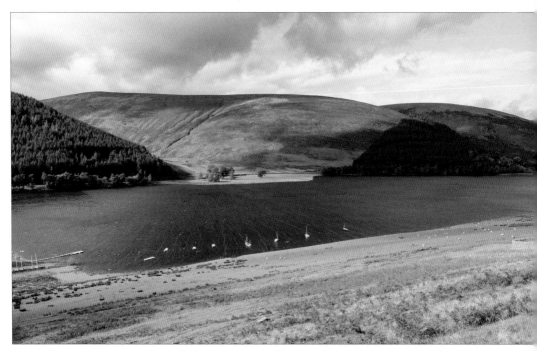

46 And so to St Mary's Loch itself, the largest natural loch in the Borders at just over five kms/three miles long. It takes its name from a church dedicated to St Mary that once stood on the northern shore.

Immediately south of St Mary's Loch is the smaller but equally lovely Loch of the Lowes, 47
seen here on an autumn evening.

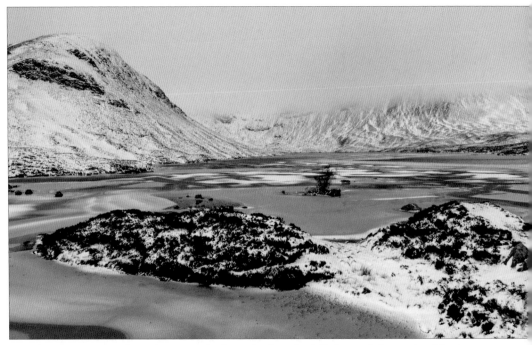

48 The snow comes: this is frozen Loch Skeen, high in the hills beyond the Loch of the Lowes, actually just over in Dumfriesshire, but a scene typical of these parts in winter.

The minor road west from Cappercleuch to Tweedsmuir takes in some dramatic scenery, especially where it passes Talla Linn falls. A series of cascades, like this one, sees the burn drop hundreds of feet in total.

50 The burn feeds Talla Reservoir, pictured here from near the top of the falls on a windy day that produced rapidly changing patterns of light and shade.

Misty morning light begins to illuminate the countryside between Broughton and Biggar. This is the **51** western limit of the Borders – the more distant ridges are in South Lanarkshire.

52 A northerly hop takes us to the picturesque village of West Linton. This is a corner of The Green with the Olde Toll Tea House in the foreground and St Andrew's Church beyond.

Not far from Peebles, Dawyck Botanic Garden offers many horticultural treats, including carpets of **53**
snowdrops in February. Since 1979 Dawyck has been in the care of the Royal Botanic Garden Edinburgh.

54 En route from Dawyck to Peebles, Neidpath Castle can be seen in its commanding position on the banks of the Tweed. The L-plan castle dates back to the 14th century.

Peebles benefits from an idyllic setting and has been developed in a manner which makes the most **55** of its natural gifts, as this picture of the parkland by the Tweed demonstrates.

56 Peebles is surrounded by hills that offer a number of great walks. For example, the 15-mile Dun Rig Horseshoe takes in the four peaks surrounding Glensax with extensive views like this one in all directions.

58 Even a winter night in Peebles can make for a striking image, with the floodlit Old Parish Church standing tall above the fast-flowing river.

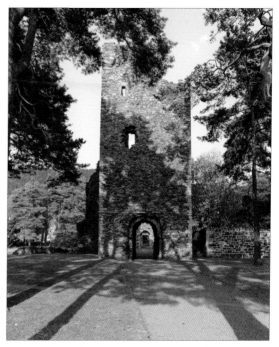

Left: this stained glass window in the Old Parish Church beautifully illustrates local scenes. **59**
Right: Cross Kirk tower, the centrepiece of the ruins of a church complex begun in the late 1100s.

60 Peebles is a busy town with a High Street full of characterful architecture. Among many points of interest are the Tweeddale Museum and Gallery and the unusually elaborate War Memorial.

Kailzie Gardens are situated two miles east of Peebles. As well as the gardens themselves, a variety of **61** other activities can be enjoyed, including osprey-watching and fishing. This is one of the fishponds.

62 This is the view north from Kailzie Gardens across the Tweed and up to the hills beyond. The contrast between the heather-clad moors and the geometric stands of timber adds interest to the vista.

Continuing to the south-east, our next destination is Innerleithen. Pictured just north of the town, **63** this is Leithen Water, the source of which rises in the Moorfoot Hills.

THE RELIANCE,
FIELDHOUSE, ELLIOTT, & Co.
OTLEY.

64 One of Innerleithen's attractions is the preserved Robert Smail's Printing Works. Visitors can see the printing presses in action and try their hand at traditional typesetting.

Also not to be missed in Innerleithen is St Ronan's Well Visitor Centre. This historic spa hosts exhibitions telling the story of the town and St Ronan's Well.

66 Just to the south of Innerleithen is the wonderful Traquair House which has the distinction of being Scotland's oldest inhabited residence. Dating back to 1107, it was originally a royal hunting lodge.

An excellent way to continue from Traquair is along the Southern Upland Way long distance walk,
which goes over the hills via the Three Brethren boundary cairns, built in the 1500s.

68 South of the Three Brethren, in the valley of Yarrow Water, stands Bowhill. This house of unique grandeur is the Scottish Borders home of the Duke of Buccleuch KBE.

Left: in Selkirk, the statue of Sir Walter Scott stands in front of the old courthouse. He served as Sherriff of Selkirkshire from 1800 to 1832. Right: statue of the explorer Mungo Park, from Selkirkshire too.

70 Also in Selkirk, this is Halliwell's House Museum. It recreates the building's former use as a home and an ironmonger's shop and also tells the story of the historic burgh of Selkirk.

The Halliwell name remains active in present-day retailing, as this award-winning butcher's shop in Selkirk shows. It also typifies how Borders towns retain a high proportion of independent shops.

72 We backtrack briefly to enjoy this Tweed Valley panorama taken from Laverlaw, east of Peebles, which can be seen in the distance. One of the Kailzie Gardens' ponds can just be seen in the reground, left of centre. All in all, a wonderful view.

74 Sir Walter Scott is the greatest literary figure associated with the Borders. He designed and built his magnificent home, Abbotsford, overlooking the Tweed just outside Galashiels.

Sir Walter Scott's kitchen garden is where the vegetables and fruit needed to feed his household were grown. Today this delightful walled garden provides a more floral feast.

76 Galashiels is another textile town that has diversified in more recent times. Cornmill Fountain makes use of the old lade from a demolished corn mill and forms this water feature in front of the Burgh Chambers

Bank Street Gardens provide a pleasant place to relax. Galashiels is built on the banks of Gala Water
about a mile from its confluence with the Tweed.

78 Handsome Old Gala House in Galashiels is a composite building that has been added to and altered over a period of more than 400 years. It has been a museum since 1988. One of the permanent

exhibitions tells the story of the house, episodes of which are depicted in the two murals, above left. **79**
Right: the Painted Ceiling Room retains the intricate patterns applied to the ceiling beams.

80 The Borders Railway opened in 2015, a 30-mile route from Tweedbank to Edinburgh that re-established part of the former 'Waverley' line. Here, a train calls at Galashiels.

The Borders are famous for the 'Common Ridings', the centrepiece of each one being a ceremonial rideout around local boundaries. This is the Galashiels event, known as the Braw Lads' Day.

82 Another short hop east brings us to the lovely town of Melrose, set at the foot of the Eildon Hills, from the top of which we look down on the town and surrounding area.

Descending from North Eildon Hill for a closer look, this is Melrose Market Place with the **83**
Mercat Cross on the right. Melrose is a lovely base from which to explore the Borders.

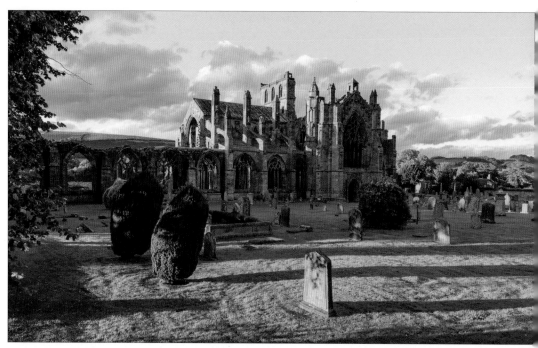

84 Melrose Abbey is a magnificent ruin on a grand scale. It was founded in 1136 by Cistercian monks at the request of King David I. It is also the burial place of Robert the Bruce's heart.

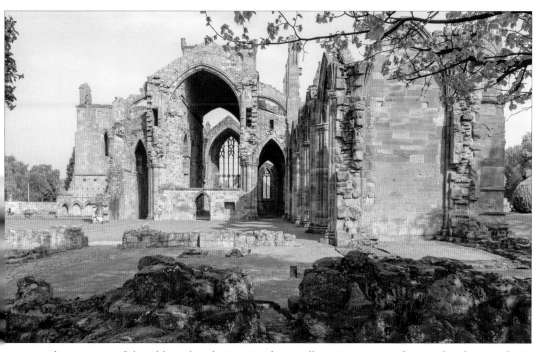

The anatomy of the Abbey church: its ruined state allows inspection of internal and external features simultaneously. Despite the devastation, much delicate stonework remains.

86 To the north of the church extensive remnants show the layout of other parts of the abbey. These are the footings of the Lay Brothers range with the Commendator's (Abbot's) House on the right.

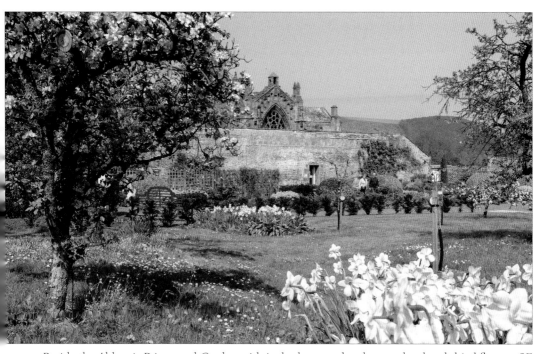

Beside the Abbey is Priorwood Garden with its herbaceous borders, orchard and dried flower **87** garden. The nearby Harmony Garden is also worth a visit while in Melrose.

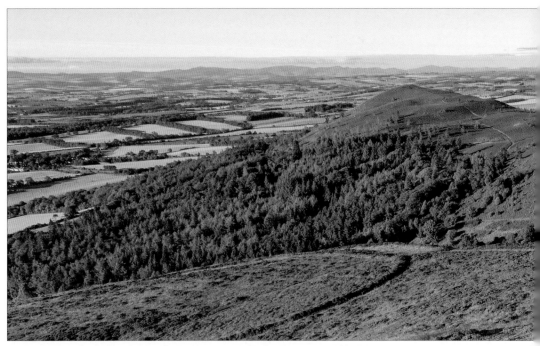

88 An exploration of the Eildon Hills makes an excellent and worthwhile half-day walk from the centre of Melrose. Their Roman name 'trimontium' is a clue to there being three summits in all.

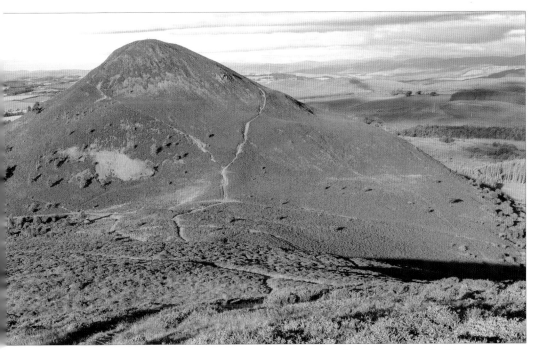

his view looks south-west from North Eildon Hill to Eildon Mid Hill on the right and Eildon Vester Hill to the left.

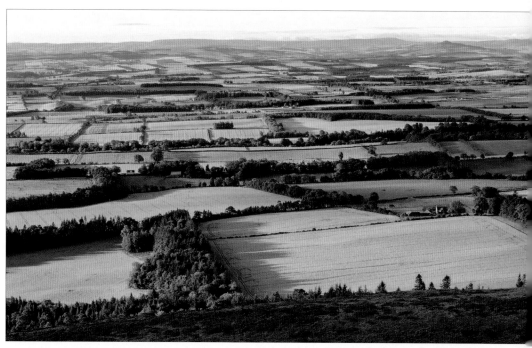

90 The views from the Eildons are so fine it's hard to choose which ones to include. Here, soon after sunrise on a summer day, the landscape to the south shows off the region's agricultural richness.

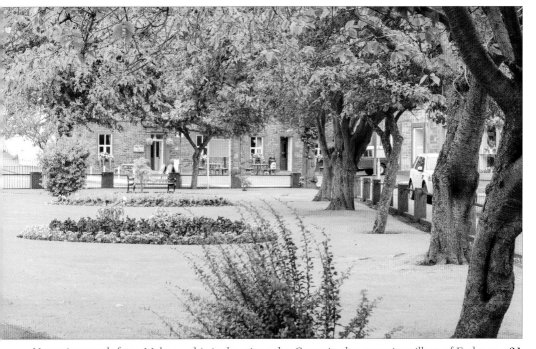

Venturing north from Melrose, this is the triangular Green in the attractive village of Earlston. **91**
A settlement since the 1200s, what is seen today is a planned layout from the 1700s.

92 Continuing a northerly trajectory brings us to Thirlestane Castle. It is a first-class example of how what began as a fort in the 13th century has evolved into a stately home of unique appearance.

These pictures of the State Dining and Drawing Rooms demonstrate the palatial qualities of the **93** Maitland family home. The castle has undergone restoration recently to safeguard its future.

94 Thirlestane Castle is situated on the edge of the small town of Lauder where the Old Parish Church is unique. It is the only cruciform church with an octagonal central tower in Scotland.

Returning southwards provides an opportunity to enjoy the iconic Scott's View, one of Sir Walter's favourites. With the River Tweed in the foreground, the distant Eildon Hills inevitably draw the eye.

96 Not far from Scott's View is the extensive village of St Boswells. The Green, seen here, is said to be the largest village green in Scotland. The village's name derives from St Boisil, an abbot of Melrose.

Smailholm Tower is a remarkably well-preserved fortified home built in the first half of the 15th century. It stands on a prominent ridge-top location a few miles east of St Boswells.

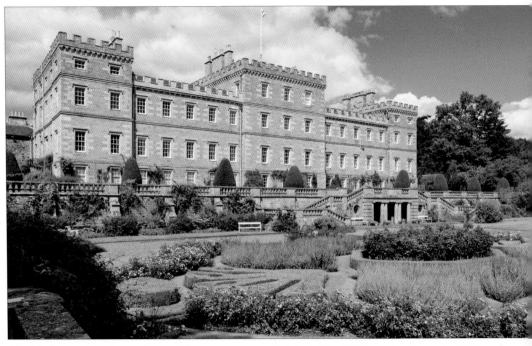

98 Rome wasn't built in a day and the same can certainly be said of Mellerstain. Begun in 1725 and completed in 1778, this grand stately home has a fascinating history and is of unique architectural interest

Having travelled north-east from Mellerstain, this is Market Square in the town of Duns. It served as the county town of Berwickshire after Berwick itself ended up in England from 1482.

100 Historic 14th-century Duns Castle is situated in the rolling hills, fields and forests of the Borders on the edge of the little market town of Duns. It is privately owned but available for functions.

In the hills north of Duns is Edin's Hall Broch. Brochs were Iron-Age stone roundhouses mainly **101** found in the north-west of Scotland, so the presence of a broch in this locality is curious.

102 The home of Lord Palmer, Manderston is the Edwardian House *par excellence*. It was built with no expense spared and with every modern convenience of that era. It can be found just east of Duns.

We now return to the Borders coast where the port of Eyemouth is full of interest such as the fort on **103** the right, to the left of which is Gunsgreen House where visitors can discover the secrets of smuggling.

104 Spectacular coastal scenery around the village of St Abbs. Although the village was only developed from 1833, its name is derived from a Northumbrian princess of long ago: Aebbe founded a

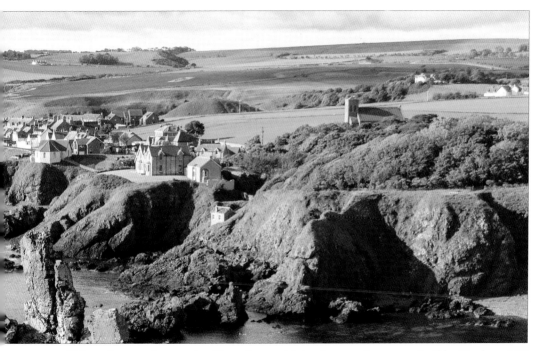

monastery c.635 on the coast just north of here, hence this has become known as St Abbs Head
nd the village took the same name. Today this area is a National Nature Reserve.

106 Long ago, smuggling was big business in these parts. Eyemouth Maritime Centre, pictured here, has a feature on smuggling as part of its remit of telling the story of mankind afloat.

Eyemouth remains a busy fishing port – this boat is about to land its catch. The harbour is home to a wide range of vessels and has an active boat repair yard, so a walk around it is always rewarding.

108 The pretty village of Coldingham is just north of Eyemouth. Coldingham Priory is the still-impressive remnant of a much larger complex that was founded c.1098 at the request of King Edgar.

Coldingham Sands: the joy of a beach at the break of day! **109**

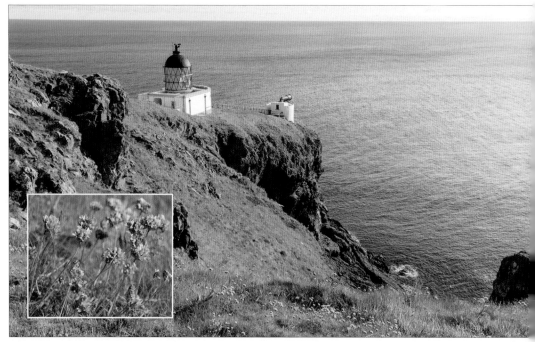

110 St Abbs Head Lighthouse is one of the principal lights in Scotland and marks the southern entrance to the Firth of Forth. Inset: Sea Thrift grows abundantly here.

The bay by the northern tip of St Abbs Head is known as Pettico Wick. From here we look north 111
towards the Lothians – but that's another journey and another book . . .

Published 2017 by Lyrical Scotland, an imprint of Lomond Books Ltd, Broxburn, EH52 5NF
www.lyricalscotland.com www.lomondbooks.com

Originated by Ness Publishing, 47 Academy Street, Elgin, Moray, IV30 1LR
(1st edition 2012, reprinted 2014, 2nd edition 2016 published by Ness Publishing)

Printed in China

All photographs © Colin & Eithne Nutt except p.14 © The Paxton Trust; p.28 © Monteviot House;
p.36 © Guthrie Aerial Photography; pp.56/57, 67 & 109 © Keith Fergus; p.68 © Bowhill Country Estate;
p.81 © Grant Kinghorn; p.93 (both) © Thirlestane Castle; p.100 © Duns Castley

Text © Colin Nutt
ISBN 978-1-78818-008-5

Front cover: Dryburgh Abbey; p.1: rainbow over St Abbs church; p.4: a young alpaca in the grounds
of Barony Castle Hotel; this page: fishing boat off St Abbs Head; back cover: Leaderfoot viaduct near Melrose,
a monument to a long-abandoned railway line